Arena of Laughter

Political Cartoons from India.. today

Vol. 2

Sudheer Nath
(Sudhi)

India Research Press
New Delhi

Published by

TARA press

mass market division

India Research Press

B-4/22, Safdarjung Enclave, New Delhi – 110 029. Ph.: 4694610; Fax : 4618637

www.indiaresearch press.com, e-mail : bahrisons@vsnl.com

2002

ISBN : 81-87943-32-7 (Vol.2)

Cataloging in Publication Data

SUDHEER NATH

Arena of Laughter-Political Cartoons from India....today

by Sudheer Nath

Includes bibliographical references and index.

1. Politics 2. Cartoons 3. India 4. Title.

Printed in India by Focus Impressions, New Delhi – 110 003.

India Research Press

B-4/22, Safdarjung Enclave, New Delhi – 110 029 Ph.: 4694610 Fax : 4618637

www.indiaresearch press.com, e-mail : bahrisons@vsnl.com

In memory of my father

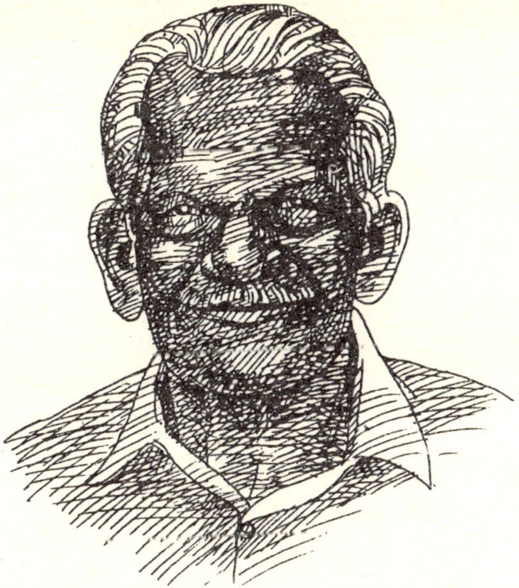

Dr. M. Babunathan
(1924 - 2001)

Foreword

Sudheer Nath is yet another link in the long chain of cartoonists from Kerala who have won themselves an audience in the North. It is not surprising that the cartoon that is a visual jibe, comment or aphorism, is best developed in India's most literate state. Indeed, if language emerged out of signs then the cartoon emerges as a sign out of the concepts a well-developed language plays with.

The element of playing with visual images to make them radiate ideas that may be very different from them - is what makes a cartoon memorable. For example, he uses the visual ploy of the spider's web with Jaya Jaitley and Bangaru Laxman caught in it (with an obvious visual pun on the words 'web' and 'net' to remind one of Tehelka.com) and is able to show it as extending to the Defence Minister, George Fernandes, the Prime Minister's Office or the BJP, who are all caught up in a damage control exercise to save their skins. Also, the use of a black background for the area within the web evokes the concept of all those involved in the process being tarred with the same brush.

When one begins to unravel the ramifications of an image like this, one cannot help but appreciate how concise and pithy a cartoon is as visual expression. In the same way, one is struck by the manner in which he uses the image of the Finance Minister walking off with the letter 'T' from between the 'U' and 'I' of the Unit Trust of India, leaving a gap of trust between the Finance Minister (represented by 'U') and the common man as 'I'. Here, very subtly, the artist identifies himself with the common man and distances himself from the Government he cannot trust after the UTI scam.

It is by his spontaneity and subtlety that Sudheer draws one towards the nuances, his images introduce one to. This is a character he shares with yet another cartoonist, Shankar. Indeed, the fact that his cartoons remind one of the redoubtable Shankar, with their simplicity and spontaneity, is perhaps the best compliment one can pay his work.

.....and when one learns that he uses a mouse for a brush, one can see him moving with his times so will go a long way from here.

Suneet Chopra
Art critic and writer

Acknowledgements

My journey from the suburbs of Kochi to the mega city of dreams.."Delhi" has been a struggle worth remembering. I am thankful to all my friends who had at one stage or the other given me good advice and helped me in finding direction towards my destination.

In this vast city of remembrance, I am grateful to my friends and fellow cartoonists - who encouraged me in times when I had no work and the struggles limitless.

Just to name a few -Sukumar, Kutty,Yesudas, Unni, Nathan, M.S.Mohanachandran,Padma Shree V.K.Madhavan Kutty, T.V.R.Shenoy, D.Vijaymohan, Appukuttan Vallikunnu, Vasudevan Anthikkadu, Sunit Chopra, Sitaram Yachuri, K.P.Unnikrishnan and Sudhakaran.

My special thanks to the Kerala Cartoon Academy & Spark Research Centre-Kochi, Observer Business & Politics, Deshabhimani, Lok Lahar, Peoples Democracy, Pakkanar, Hasya Kairali, MEANTIME, JAAL.MAG.COM, ARTINDIA.NET

Thanks are also due to my friend Subodh Kaura, who took the initiative to introduce me to Anuj Bahri, the publisher of my books "Arena of Laughter".

Sudheer Nath

Publishers Note

Not long ago did I have the pleasure of meeting Sudheer at my office... when he walked in clutching a stack of papers in his hands, not knowing what to say. He placed himself on a chair - waiting. He had a recommendation from a mutual friend and I thought of granting him the standard 10 minutes that all busy pulishers are obliged to give.

After speaking to him for a few minutes, I realized the need for us to invest in this unknown cartoonist. His style - free flowing so possessed me, that I made up my mind instantly to do a series of his work under our imprint of Tara.

I must confess of the unsure times when I wanted to just stop this project, but something in these images full of life and humor, kept me going.

It is ironic how most of the cartoonists contributing to the Indian humor and caricature family orginate, or at some time in life - have been attached to Kerala, but I found something different in sudheer s style that we have today collected in these volumes for you to enjoy....!!

Anuj Bahri Malhotra

NDA
SUDHI

LOOK AT HER FATHER; VOTE FOR HER
LOOK AT HIS MOTHER; VOTE FOR HIM
LOOK AT ME AND ELECT MY MUMMY
SUDHI

BUDGET
SUDHI

VIDESHI
?
SWADESHI
?
SUDHI

SHE IS STILL IN THE SILLY POINT.....
SUDHI

I ROLLED BACK
OH MY GOODNESS
I'M LOGGING OUT
MAMATA
MATH

?
VOTE FOR A STABLE GOVERNMENT ONCE AGAIN
NATH

FOR SALE
SUDHI

...LIGHT'S ON...
CAMARA....
ACTION...
UF PRODECTION
TAKE-2
DIRECTOR
BUDGET
SUDHEER NATH

PLEASE HOLD THE LANTERN A LITTLE TO YOUR LEFT
WE DON'T GET ENOUGH LIGHTS FROM YOUR LANTERN COMRADE
I CAN'T SEE THE WAY PROPERLY..
CPI
SUDHI

AICC
AM I CORRECT
NO... NEVER....MAM
YOU ARE NOT
CORRUPT....
SUDHI

...THEN WHERE WILL WE ALL FIND SPACE..?
A BIG SMALL CAR!!
SUDHI

HALLOO ....
HALLOO ......
SAY, YES
YES
NO
NO
NATH

AGAIN MAMATA DRAMA....!!
A 'ROLLED BACK' STORY...
MADAM.....
A WELL WISHER HAS
SEND THIS GIFT.....
RESIGNATION
XEROX
MACHINE
NATH

DOCTOR

BUDDIES...
THIS IS YOUR NEWLY DESIGNED ONE....
UMA BHART
INDIA
IND
CRICKET TEAM
ICC
NATH

KARGIL
SUDHI

SORRY DEAR
MY REMOTE IS
NOT WORKING
OOHHHH.....
OHHHH...
HH..
SUDHEER

5 Year Guarantee 5 year
NDA ALLIES
RSS ISSUE

BIHAR EXPRESS
SUDHEER

HAI RAM.....!!...
FROM US
NATH

NOW YOU ALL ARE WATCHING CTBT DRAMA DIRECTED BY BILL
SUDHIR

543 SEATS
VALUED UP TO 2025

CREDIT POLICY
FOREX POLICY
SUDHI

OIL POOL
DEFICIT
IT WILL
COME DOWN
EVENTUALLY
FOLKS
CPM
SUDHEER

QUIT BJP
QUIT HUNG PARLIAMENT
QUIT INDIA QUIT INDIA QUIT INDIA
THE RIGHT PERSON FOR EXTERNAL AFFIARS
SUDHEER

BIFR →
AAIFR →
SUDHI

BUDGET
IT'S HALF BAKED
HOW WILL IT GO DOWN WITH THE POOR
IT NEEDS TO BE SLICED
SUDHEER NATH

WHO IS OUR
FATHER OF NATION...?

HANDLE
WITH
CARE
SUDHI

WE DON'T BOTHER ABOUT SWADESHI OR VIDESHI TASTE... WE NEED A STABLE GOVERNMENT...
SUDHI

....AND THE NEXT ITEM IN OUR AGENDA IS....

PO
TO
POT
MATH

NEXT TIME YOU CAN EXPECT MORE NUKES... MORE WAR.. AND... MORE MORE...
JAY ~~SREERAM~~ KARGIL
JAY JAY
NATH

SUDHI.

BALCO
INDIA
2001 BUDGET
INDIAN AIRLINES
AIR INDIA
TAX
NATH

OIL POOL
....TEN.... NINE....EIGHT...
SUDHEER NATH

GROOPISUM IS THE SECRET OF OUR ENERGY
SCAM IS THE SECRET OF MY ENERGY
NATIONAL POLITICAL GAMES '97
SUDHEER NATH

CURRENCY-WARD

MAHARASHTRA CONTRAVERCY
CAUVERY CONTRAVERCY
VAJPAYEE GOVERNMENT
NATH

ARRAI...THHOOO...
MAKE CLEAR
OUR WAY.....
VHP ॐ
SAVE
RAM RAJYA
SAVE
OUR
SECULAR
INDIA
NATH

FROGS IN THE WELL.....
269+
14
283
283-
272
11
SUDHI

.... WHO'S NEXT....?
NATH

NOTHING BUT SUPPORT TO MY FORMER LEADER...
SUDHI

BAAP RE...!!
HUMAN BOMB...!!
VOTE FOR
SUDHEER

AT LAST I ADMIT
NATH

PUBLIC
PUBLIC
NATH

DEAR BILL DONT USE THIS TYPE OF WEAPON AGAIN.....
SUDHI

USE ONE HAND FOR THAT....
REWRITE THIS TOO.....
POTO
HISTORY
SUDHI

THIS ONE, WE CAN SEND BY THE DELHI-LAHORE BUS......
MAYA

EC FREEZER
OUR CHARKKAAA....
LET'S WAIT FOR IT TO DEFROST....
NCP
CONGRESS(S)
HOW WILL WE ALLOT SYMBOLS?
PICTURE
BIRDS OF INDIA
PICTURES OF TOOLS
OUR ANIMALS
TO EC OFFICE
THEY ARE READY TO ALLY WITH ANYONE...; EXCEPT TELEPHONE SYMBOL HOLDERS...
BJP
VOTE SELECT
SUDHI

ANY MORE
MASALA....
CM
SUDHEER NATH

KARGIL
LEFTOSCOPE
BEJEPEYOSCOPE
CONGROSCOPE
SUDHI

POLITICAL EVOLUTION
SWADESHI
SWADESHI PRIME
SWADESHI PRIME MINISTER
?!
NATH

ONLY TEN AT A TIME
CO ORDINATION COMMITTEE

WE PROUDLY PRESENT....
.....
AICC

THE GREAT ECONOMIC HURDLE....
BUDG
FIRST AID BOX
NATH

WELCOME TO MILLENIUM WORLD PEACE SUMMIT
NEW YO
NO ENTRY TO DALAI LAMA
FROM, INDIA
NATH

BABRI
CASE

BAD DREAMS
SOMEBODY
COMING TO
KILL US...
P.M

SORRY DEAR...
I CAN ALSO FEEL
YOUR'S PAIN...
ELECTION
'98
SUDHEER

JAYA IN THE WONDER LAND
PM
....THEN WHAT HAPPENED TO MY CALCULATION..?

NATIONAL ~~DEMOCRATIC~~
SCAM
ALLIANCE (N ~~D~~ A)
S
NATH

SHILANYAS
GUJARAT GOVT
HOME MINISTR
NATH

WE WILL DECIDE LATER HOW TO PLAY IN THIS GROUND WITH THESE '13' BATS
NDA
SAD
BJP
NATH

BOMBAY BOYS... NEXT YOU BRING SOME CLOTHES TO HIDE MY ....
BCCI
HINDUTVA TUB
NATH

JAYALALITHA IN TOWN
SEVERE QUAKE
ROCKS
NORTH.....
SUDHI

STEERING WITH ME, BILL...
BUT.... BRAKE, CLUTCH AND
GEAR WITH
MUJAHIDEENS..
US
SUDHI

BJP
PRESS
NATH

ONCE AGAIN YOU MUST SUPPORT ME.... OTHERWISE WE CAN'T GET SUPPORT FROM OUT SIDE...
SUDHEER

INDIAN
CORPORATE
MARKET
SUPPLY
SUDHI

POLITICAL
LIFTING
INDIA
DEAR....
THIS IS FOR
YOUR VICTORY
US DRUGS
NATH

FIR
FIRE
DY: SPEAKER = R.M. SAYED..
HALOOO.
IS'T FIRE STATION..
NATH

NO..SIGN
OF LIFE
OVER... OVER..
BJP
GOVERNMENT
SUDHI

EDUCATE THE PEOPLE ABOUT GOVERMENT'S HARD DECISIONS :- VAJPAYEE

NATH

ADJOURN
THE LOK SABHA
SINE DIE

SONIA JI IS THE SECRET OF MY ENERGY..!!
10 JANPATH
IN
CONGRESS
....AT LAST IT HAS BECOME A REAL TITANIC....!!
NATH

'Q'
10
RUNNING FOR TICKET WITH 'DD'
'Q'
10
WAITING FOR A REPLY
HUNGAMA
SCRATCH HERE
HUNGAMA
TRY AGAIN
BEST OF LUCK
-AICC-
SUDHI

SWADESHI CUM VIDESHI
FINANCE MINISTER

NATH

THE REMOTE DOLL
INDIA

SUDHI

PRICE RESTRAINT
GROWTH RESTRAINT
SUDHI

... LET US TAKE A CUP OF TATA TEA...
VEERAPPAN
SUDHEER

TATA
VSNL
INDIAN
PUBLIC
SECTOR
NATH

HELP
HELP
HELP
HELP
HELP
SUDHEER

OUR SYMBOL
OUR SYMBOL
OUR SYMBOL
OUR SYMBOL
OUR SYMBOL
SUDHEER

NOT ONLY THE CONSTITUTION WE PLANNED TO REVIEW ALL BOOKS....
GITA
MAHABHARATA
RAMAYANAM
INDIAN CONSTITUTION
NATH

MAM....
I'M (WE) ARE
YOUR SEVAK...
SELF
CERTIFIED
SWAYAMSEVEK
: VAJPAYE
REPORT
MAMATA
NATH

AUTONOMY PROROSAL
103
104
105
106
NATH

INDIAN WORM....

INDIAN HIS
JOSHI SUGGESTS
REWRITING
HISTORY
:— NEWS —.
MATH

YEHI HAI RIGHT CHOICE...
COKE
PEPSI
PEPSI
COKE
NATH

SUDHEER NATH

HALOOOO
DOT
ZZZZZzz
SUDHI

CM
U
P
SUDHI

SATI MATA KI JAI
SATI KE PATI KI JAI
INDIAN DEMOCRACY
DIESEL
NATH

...HAI....
ONE MORE EXPECTATION
I'VE FROM YOUR SIDE....
A PARLAMENT SEAT
PHOOLAN DEVI GETS
PARLIAMENT SEAT....

..EUREKA..EUREKA..
AYODHYA EXPLOSIVE
NATH

DON'T UTTER ANYTHING NOW....
YES, YOU ARE TRYING
TO WISH US A....
HAPPY AND A....
PROSPEROUS....
NEW YEAR....
SUDHI

YESTERDAY
....
KISSA KURSI KA...?

....AND THE DAY AFTER..
SUDHI

KARGIL
SUDHI

START POINT
START POINT
IT'S RIGHT.... THE WORLD IS ROUND...
SUDHI.

WORST BENGAL
JUNGLE BENGAL
NO OTHER WAY TO LIVE.. IN BENGAL..
PANJA.... DID ANY ONE CALL.... ....REMIND.... WE WANT POWER...
RAILWAYS
EXTERNAL AFFAIRS
HIKE IN PETROL PRICES...
NATH

WE MUST DISGUSS ABOUT OUR SYMBOL SERIOUSLY
OUR SYMBOL
NATH

INTEREST RATES
SUDHI

CAN WE SEND ONE MORE LETTER ?
THAKKAR
BOFORS
SUDHEER

SUDHI

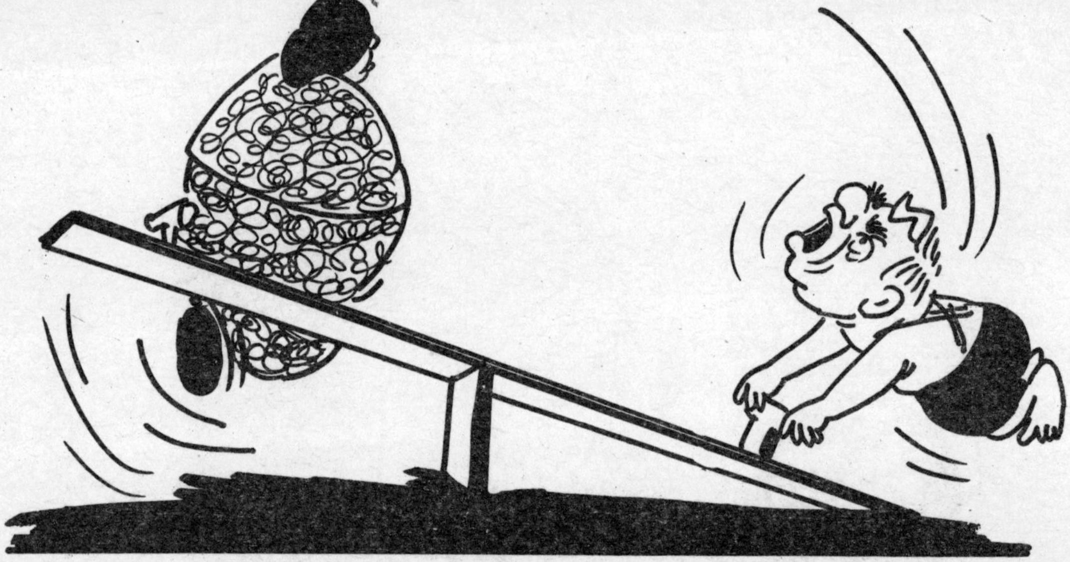

COLLEGE
FOR TOMORROWS FUTURE....
VOTE FOR ME
UNEMPLOY
SUDHI

BE CHEERFULL.. DEAR.... LIFE is LIKE ONION.... IT'S VALUE GOES UP AND DOWN..
NATH

OT FOR WHAT
VOTE FOR WHAT WHOME
WHOME OR WHAT..?
FOR WHAT WHOME
SUDHEER

LAW

WORLD CUP 98
LIVE
OUR LOTUS IS SHOWING THERE ALSO.... NOTHING BUT IT'S THE IMPACT OF POKHRAN
11/6/98 SUDHEER

AYODHYA...!?
NATH

VAJPAYEE WRITES SHORT STORY FOR CHILDREN :News Item

AT LAST BLESSINGS GOES TO ....
POOR CONGRESS..!! ...
MATH

....IS THERE ANY NEED OF COUNTDOWN HERE....
AGNI II
NATH

RAJYA SABHA
RESOLUTION
Soo.....
Sooo..
Sooo..
NATH

R.K. DHAWAN

MAYAWATI

RAJESH PILOT

H.D.DEVE GOWDA

NARASIMHA RAO

I.K. GUJRAL

MULAYAM SINGH

SHARAD PAWAR

For details on how to order your copy of cartoons..... check last page.

CHANDRA BABU NAIDU

BANSI LAL

L.K. ADVANI

SHARAD YADAV

MADHU DANDAUATDE

MADAN LAL KHURANA

V.C. SHUKLA

SITA RAM KESRI

For details on how to order your copy of cartoons..... check last page.

K. KARUNAKARAN

P. CHIDHAMBARAM

KALYAN SINGH

JYOTI BASU

E.K. NAYANAR

N KARUNANIDHI

MS GILL

AJIT SINGH

For details on how to order your copy of cartoons..... check last page.

MADHAV RAO SCINDIA

VN GADGIL

SITA RAM YECHURI

LALOO PRASAD YADAV

SONIA GANDHI

A.R. ANTULAY

H.S. SURJEET

C.M. IBRAHIM

For details on how to order your copy of cartoons..... check last page.

JAIPAL REDDY

PRAKASH SINGH BADAL

INDERJIT GUPTA

A.K. ANTONY

MAMTA BANERJI

MURASOLI MARAN

JAYANTI NATARAJAN

KESU BHAI PATEL

For details on how to order your copy of cartoons..... check last page.

G.K. MOOPANAR

M.P. VEERENDRA KUMAR

SATPAL MAHARAJ

And many more .... !!

All cartoons from this publication are available in original (Colour) for Rs. 500/- each.
Caricature of any person / personality can be ordered for a value of Rs. 175/- (Plus postage charges Rs. 50/- extra).... A3 size in black & white.... from :

Sudheer Nath
C/o INDIA RESEARCH PRESS
B-4/22 Safdarjung Enclave, New Delhi - 110029, India

(All payments are to be sent by MO / DD to the above address)